A Call to Prayer

A Call to Prayer

J. C. Ryle

Baker Book House
Grand Rapids, Michigan

ISBN: 0-8010-7623-4

Paperback edition issued 1976

First printing, November 1976
Second printing, August 1977
Third printing, May 1979
Fourth printing, February 1981
Fifth printing, January 1982
Sixth printing, March 1984
Seventh printing, June 1985

PHOTOLITHOPRINTED BY CUSHING - MALLOY, INC.
ANN ARBOR, MICHIGAN, UNITED STATES OF AMERICA

Men ought
always to pray.

(Luke 18:1)

I will that
men pray everywhere.

(I Tim. 2:1)

I have a question to offer you. It is contained in three words, **Do you pray?**

The question is one that none but you can answer. Whether you attend public worship or not, your minister knows. Whether you have family prayers in your house or not, your relations know. But whether you pray in private or not, is a matter between yourself and God.

I beseech you in all affection to attend to the subject I bring before you. Do not say that my question is too close. If your heart is right in the sight of God, there is nothing in it to make you afraid. Do not turn off my question by replying that you say your prayers. It is one thing to say your prayers and another to pray. Do not tell me that my question is unnecessary. Listen to me for a few minutes, and I will show you good reasons for asking it.

I ask whether you pray, because *prayer is absolutely needful to a man's salvation.*

I say, absolutely needful, and I say so advisedly. I am not speaking now of infants or idiots. I am not settling the state of the heathen. I know that where little is given, there little will be required. I speak especially of those who call themselves Christians, in a land like our own. And of such I say, no man or woman can expect to be saved who does not pray.

I hold salvation by grace as strongly as any one. I would gladly offer a free and full pardon to the greatest sinner that ever lived. I would not hesitate to stand by his dying bed, and say, "Believe on the Lord Jesus Christ even now, and you shall be saved." But that a man can have salvation without *asking* for it, I cannot see in the Bible. That a man will receive pardon of his sins, who will not so much as lift up his heart inwardly, and say, "Lord Jesus, give it to me," this I cannot find. I can find that nobody will be saved by his prayers, but I cannot find that without prayer anybody will be saved.

It is not absolutely needful to salvation that a man should *read* the Bible. A man may have no learning, or be blind, and yet have Christ in his heart. It is not absolutely needful that a man should hear public preaching of the gospel. He may live where the gospel is not preached, or he may be bedridden, or deaf. But the same thing cannot be said about prayer. It is absolutely needful to salvation that

11

a man should *pray*.

There is no royal road either to health or learning. Princes and kings, poor men and peasants, all alike must attend to the wants of their own bodies and their own minds. No man can eat, drink, or sleep by proxy. No man can get the alphabet learned for him by another. All these are things which everybody must do for himself, or they will not be done at all.

Just as it is with the mind and body, so it is with the soul. There are certain things absolutely needful to the soul's health and well-being. Each must attend to these things for himself. Each must repent for himself. Each must apply to Christ for himself. And for himself each must speak to God and pray. You must do it for yourself, for by nobody else can it be done.

To be prayerless is to be without God, without Christ, without grace, without hope, and without heaven. It is to be on the road to hell. Now can you wonder that I ask the question, **Do you pray?**

I ask again whether you pray, because *a habit of prayer is one of the surest marks of a true Christian.*

All the children of God on earth are alike in this respect. From the moment there is any life and reality about their religion, they pray. Just as the first sign of life in an infant when born into the world is the act of breathing, so the first act of men and women when they are born again is *praying.*

This is one of the common marks of all the elect of God, "They cry unto him day and night" (Luke 18:1). The Holy Spirit, who makes them new creatures, works in them the feeling of adoption, and makes them cry, "Abba, Father" (Rom. 8:15). The Lord Jesus, when he quickens them, gives them a voice and a tongue, and says to them, "Be dumb no more." God has no dumb children. It is as much a part of their new nature to pray, as it is of a child to cry. They see their need of mercy and grace. They feel their emptiness and weakness. They cannot do otherwise than they do. They *must* pray.

I have looked carefully over the lives of God's saints in the Bible. I cannot find one of whose history much is told us, from Genesis to Revelation, who was not a man of prayer. I find it mentioned as a characteristic of the godly, that "they call on the Father" (I Peter 1:17), or "the name of the Lord Jesus Christ" (I Cor. 1:2). Recorded as a characteristic of the wicked is the fact that "they call not upon the Lord" (Ps. 14:4).

I have read the lives of many eminent Christians who have been on earth since the Bible days. Some of them, I see, were rich, and some poor. Some were learned, and some unlearned. Some of them were Episcopalians, and some Christians of other names. Some were Calvinists, and some were Arminians. Some have loved to use a liturgy, and some to use none. But one thing, I see, they all had in common. They have all been *men of prayer*.

I study the reports of missionary societies in our own times. I see with joy that heathen men and women are receiving the gospel in various parts of the globe. There are conversions in Africa, in New Zealand, in Hindustan, in China. The people converted are naturally unlike one another in every respect. But one striking thing I observe at all the missionary stations: the converted people *always pray*.

I do not deny that a man may pray without heart and without sincerity. I do not for a moment pretend to say that the mere fact of a person's praying proves everything about his soul. As in every other part of religion, so also in this, there may be deception and hypocrisy.

But this I do say, that not praying is a clear proof that a man is not yet a true Christian. He cannot really feel his sins. He cannot love God. He cannot feel himself a debtor to Christ. He cannot long after holiness. He cannot desire heaven. He has yet to be born again. He has yet to be made a new creature. He may boast confidently of election, grace, faith, hope, and knowledge, and deceive ignorant people. But you may rest assured it is all vain talk *if he does not pray*.

And I say, furthermore, that of all the evidences of the real work of the Spirit, a habit of hearty private prayer is one of the most satisfactory that can be named. A man may preach from false motives. A man may write books and make fine speeches and seem diligent in good works, and yet be a Judas Iscariot. But a man seldom goes into his closet, and pours out his soul before God in secret, unless he is in earnest. The Lord himself has set his stamp on prayer as the best proof of a true conversion. When he sent Ananias to Saul in Damascus, he gave him no other evidence of his change of heart than this, *"Behold, he prayeth"* (Acts 9:11).

I know that much may go on in a man's mind before he is brought to pray. He may have many convictions, desires, wishes, feelings, intentions, resolutions, hopes, and fears. But all these things are very uncertain evidences. They are to be found in ungodly people, and often come to nothing. In many a case they are not more lasting than the morning cloud, and the dew that passeth away. A real, hearty prayer, coming from a broken and contrite spirit, is worth all these things put together.

I know that the Holy Spirit, who calls sinners from their evil ways, does in many instances lead them by very slow degrees to acquaintance with Christ. But the eye of man can only judge by what it sees. I cannot call any one justified until he believes. I dare not say that any one believes until he prays. I cannot understand a dumb faith. The first act of faith will be to speak to God. Faith is to the soul what life is to the body. Prayer is to faith what breath is to life. How a man can live and not breathe is past my comprehension, and how a man can believe and not pray is past my comprehension too.

Never be surprised if you hear ministers of the gospel dwelling much on the importance of prayer. This is the point we want to bring you to; we want to know that you pray. Your views of doctrine may be correct. Your love of Protestantism may be warm and unmistakable. But still this may be nothing more than head knowledge and party spirit. We want to know whether you are actually acquainted with the throne of grace, and whether you can speak *to* God as well as speak *about* God.

Do you wish to find out whether you are a true Christian? Then rest assured that my question is of the very first importance — **Do you pray?**

I ask whether you pray, because *there is no duty in religion so neglected as private prayer.*

We live in days of abounding religious profession. There are more places of public worship now than there ever were before. There are more persons attending them than there ever were before. And yet in spite of all this public religion, I believe there is a vast neglect of private prayer. It is one of those private transactions between God and our souls which no eye sees, and therefore one which men are tempted to pass over and leave undone.

I believe that thousands *never utter a word of prayer at all*. They eat. They drink. They sleep. They rise. They go forth to their labor. They return to their homes. They breathe God's air. They see God's sun. They walk on God's earth. They enjoy God's mercies. They have dying bodies. They have judgment and eternity before them. But they *never speak to God*. They live like the beasts that perish. They behave like creatures without souls. They have not one word to say to Him in whose hand are their life and breath, and all things, and from whose mouth they must one day receive their everlasting sentence. How dreadful this seems; but if the secrets of men were only known, how common.

I believe there are tens of thousands *whose prayers are nothing but a mere form*, a set of words repeated by rote, without a thought about their meaning.

Some say over a few hasty sentences picked up in the nursery when they were children. Some content themselves with repeating the Creed, forgetting that there is not a request in it. Some add the Lord's Prayer, but without the slightest desire that its solemn petitions may be granted.

Many, even of those who use good forms, mutter their prayers after they have gotten into bed, or while they wash or dress in the morning. Men may think what they please, but they may depend upon it that in the sight of God *this is not praying*. Words said without heart are as utterly useless to our souls as the drum beating of the poor heathen before their idols. Where there is *no heart*, there may be lip work and tongue work, but there is nothing that God listens to; there is *no prayer*. Saul, I have no doubt, said many a long prayer before the Lord met him on the way to Damascus. But it was not till his heart was broken that the

Lord said, "He prayeth."

Does this surprise you? Listen to me, and I will show you that I am not speaking as I do without reason. Do you think that my assertions are extravagant and unwarrantable? Give me your attention, and I will soon show you that I am only telling you the truth.

Have you forgotten that it is *not natural* to any one to pray? "The carnal mind is enmity against God." The desire of man's heart is to get far away from God, and have nothing to do with him. His feeling towards him is not love, but fear. Why then should a man pray when he has no real sense of sin, no real feeling of spiritual wants, no thorough belief in unseen things, no desire after holiness and heaven? Of all these things the vast majority of men know and feel nothing. The multitude walk in the broad way. I cannot forget this. Therefore I say boldly, I believe that few pray.

Have you forgotten that it is *not fashionable* to pray? It is one of the things that many would be rather ashamed to own. There are hundreds who would sooner storm a breach, or lead a forlorn hope, than confess publicly that they make a habit of prayer. There are thousands who, if obliged to sleep in the same room with a stranger, would lie down in bed without a prayer. To dress well, to go to theaters, to be thought clever and agreeable, all this is fashionable, but not to pray. I cannot forget this. I cannot think a habit is common which so many seem ashamed to own. I believe that few pray.

Have you forgotten *the lives that many live?* Can we really believe that people are praying against sin night and day, when we see them plunging into it? Can we suppose they pray against the world, when they are entirely absorbed and taken up with its pursuits? Can we think they really ask God for grace to serve him, when they do not show the slightest desire to serve him at all? Oh, no, it is plain as daylight that the great majority of men either ask nothing of God or *do not mean what they say* when they do ask, which is just the same thing. Praying and sinning will never live together in the same heart. Prayer will consume sin, or sin will choke prayer. I cannot forget this. I look at men's lives. I believe that few pray.

Have you forgotten *the deaths that many die?* How many, when they draw near death, seem entirely strangers to God. Not only are they sadly ignorant of his gospel, but sadly wanting in the power of speaking to him. There is a terrible awkwardness and shyness in their endeavors to approach him. They seem to be taking up a fresh thing. They appear as if they wanted an introduction to God, and as if they had never talked with him before. I remember having heard of a lady who was anxious to have a minister to visit her in her last illness. She desired that he would pray with her. He asked her what he should pray for. She did not know, and could not tell. She was utterly unable to name any one thing which she wished him to ask God for her soul. All she seemed to want was the form of a minister's prayers. I can quite understand this. Death beds are great revealers of secrets. I cannot forget what I have seen of sick and dying people. This also leads me to believe that few pray.

I cannot see your heart. I do not know your private history in spiritual things. But from what I see in the Bible and in the world I am certain I cannot ask you a more necessary question than that before you — **Do you pray?**

I ask whether you pray, because

prayer is an act in religion to which there is great encouragement.

There is everything on God's part to make prayer easy, if men will only attempt it. All things are ready on his side. Every objection is anticipated. Every difficulty is provided for. The crooked places are made straight and the rough places are made smooth. There is no excuse left for the prayerless man.

There is *a way* by which any man, however sinful and unworthy, may draw near to God the Father. Jesus Christ has opened that way by the sacrifice he made for us upon the cross. The holiness and justice of God need not frighten sinners and keep them back. Only let them cry to God in the name of Jesus, only let them plead the atoning blood of Jesus, and they shall find God upon a throne of grace, willing and ready to hear. The name of Jesus is a never-failing passport for our prayers. In that name a man may draw near to God with boldness, and ask with confidence. God has engaged to hear him. Think of this. Is not this encouragement?

There is *an Advocate* and Intercessor always waiting to present the prayers of those who come to God through him. That advocate is Jesus Christ. He mingles our prayers with the incense of his own almighty intercession. So mingled, they go up as a sweet savor before the throne of God. Poor as they are in themselves, they are mighty and powerful in the hand of our High Priest and Elder Brother. The bank note without a signature at the bottom is nothing but a worthless piece of paper. The stroke of a pen confers on it all its value. The prayer of a poor child of Adam is a feeble thing in itself, but once endorsed by the hand of the Lord Jesus it availeth much. There was an officer in the city of Rome who was appointed to have his doors always open, in order to receive any Roman citizen who applied to him for help. Just so the ear of the Lord Jesus is ever open to the cry of all who want mercy and grace. It is his office to help them. Their prayer is his delight. Think of this. Is not this encouragement?

There is *the Holy Spirit* ever ready to help our infirmities in prayer. It is one part of his special office to assist us in our endeavors to speak with God. We need not be cast down and distressed by the fear of not knowing what to say. The Spirit will give us words if we seek his aid. The prayers of the Lord's people are the inspiration of the Lord's Spirit, the work of the Holy Ghost who dwells within them as the Spirit of grace and supplication. Surely the Lord's people may well hope to be heard. It is not they merely that pray, but the Holy Ghost pleading in them. Reader, think of this. Is not this encouragement?

There are exceeding great and precious *promises* to those who pray. What did the Lord Jesus mean when he spoke such words as these· "Ask, and it shall be given you; seek, and ye shall find; knock, and it shall be opened unto you: for every one that asketh, receiveth; and he that seeketh, findeth; and to him that knocketh, it shall be opened" (Matt. 7:7, 8). "All things whatsoever ye shall ask in prayer believing, ye shall receive" (Matt. 21:22). "Whatsoever ye shall ask in my name, that will I do, that the Father may be glorified in the Son. If ye shall ask anything in my name, I will do it" (John 14:13, 14). What did the Lord mean when he spoke the parables of the friend at midnight and the importunate widow (Luke 11:5; 18:1)? Think over these passages. If this is not encouragement to pray, words have no meaning.

There are wonderful *examples* in Scripture of the power of prayer. Nothing

29

seems to be too great, too hard, or too difficult for prayer to do. It has obtained things that seemed impossible and out of reach. It has won victories over fire, air, earth, and water. Prayer opened the Red Sea. Prayer brought water from the rock and bread from heaven. Prayer made the sun stand still. Prayer brought fire from the sky on Elijah's sacrifice. Prayer turned the counsel of Ahithophel into foolishness. Prayer overthrew the army of Sennacherib. Well might Mary Queen of Scots say, "I fear John Knox's prayers more than an army of ten thousand men." Prayer has healed the sick. Prayer has raised the dead. Prayer has procured the conversion of souls. "The child of many prayers," said an old Christian to Augustine's mother, "shall never perish." Prayer, pains, and faith can do anything. Nothing seems impossible when a man has the spirit of adoption. "Let me alone," is the remarkable saying of God to Moses when Moses was about to intercede for the children of Israel — the Chaldee version has, "Leave off praying" — (Exod. 32:10). So long as Abraham asked mercy for Sodom, the Lord went on giving. He never ceased to give till Abraham ceased to pray. Think of this. Is not this encouragement?

What more can a man want to lead him to take any step in religion, than the things I have just told him about prayer? What more could be done to make the path to the mercy seat easy, and to remove all occasions of stumbling from the sinner's way? Surely if the devils in hell had such a door set open before them, they would leap for gladness, and make the very pit ring with joy.

But where will the man hide his head at last who neglects such glorious encouragements? What can possibly be said for the man who, after all, dies without prayer? Surely I may feel anxious that you should not be that man. Surely I may well ask — **Do you pray?**

I ask whether you pray, because *diligence in prayer is the secret of eminent holiness.*

Without controversy there is a vast difference among true Christians. There is an immense interval between the foremost and the hindermost in the army of God.

They are all fighting the same good fight but how much more valiantly some fight than others. They are all doing the Lord's work but how much more some do than others. They are all light in the Lord; but how much more brightly some shine than others. They are all running the same race; but how much faster some get on than others. They all love the same Lord and Saviour; but how much more some love him than others. I ask any true Christian whether this is not the case. Are not these things so?

There are some of the Lord's people who seem *never able to get on* from the time of their conversion. They are born again, but they remain babes all their lives. You hear from them the same old experience. You remark in them the same want of spiritual appetite, the same want of interest in any thing beyond their own little circle, which you remarked ten years ago. They are pilgrims, indeed, but pilgrims like the Gibeonites of old; their bread is always dry and moldy, their shoes always old, and their garments always rent and torn. I say this with sorrow and grief; but I ask any real Christian, Is it not true?

There are others of the Lord's people who seem to be *always advancing*. They grow like the grass after rain; they increase like Israel in Egypt; they press on like Gideon, though sometimes faint, yet always pursuing. They are ever adding grace to grace, and faith to faith, and strength to strength. Every time you meet them their hearts seem larger, and their spiritual stature taller and stronger. Every year they appear to see more, and know more, and believe more, and feel more in their religion. They not only have good works to prove the reality of their faith, but they are *zealous* of them. They not only do well, but they are *unwearied* in well-doing. They attempt great things, and they do great things. When they fail they try again, and when they fall they are soon up again. And all this time they think themselves poor, unprofitable servants, and fancy they do nothing at all. These are those who make religion lovely and beautiful in the eyes of all. They wrest praise even from the unconverted and win golden opinions even from the selfish men of the world.

It does one good to see, to be with, and to hear them. When you meet them, you could believe that like Moses, they had just come out from the presence of God. When you part with them you feel warmed by their company, as if your soul had been near a fire. I know such people are rare. I only ask, Are there not many such?

Now how can we account for the difference which I have just described? What is the reason that some believers are so much brighter and holier than others? I believe the difference, in nineteen cases out of twenty, arises from different habits about private prayer. I believe that those who are not eminently holy pray *little*, and those who are eminently holy pray *much*.

I dare say this opinion will startle some readers. I have little doubt that many look on eminent holiness as a kind of special gift, which none but a few must pretend to aim at. They admire it at a distance in books. They think it beautiful when they see an example near themselves. But as to its being a thing within the reach of any but a very few, such a notion never seems to enter their minds. In short, they consider it a kind of monopoly granted to a few favored believers, but certainly not to all.

Now I believe that this is a most dangerous mistake. I believe that spiritual as well as natural greatness depends in a high degree on the faithful use of means within everybody's reach. Of course I do not say we have a right to expect a miraculous grant of intellectual gifts; but this I do say, that when a man is once converted to God, his progress in holiness will be much in accordance with his own diligence in the use of God's appointed means. And I assert confidently that the principal means by which most believers have become great in the church of Christ is the habit of *diligent private prayer.*

Look through the lives of the brightest and best of God's servants, whether in the Bible or not. See what is written of Moses and David and Daniel and Paul. Mark what is recorded of Luther and Bradford the Reformers. Observe what is related of the private devotions of Whitefield and Cecil and Venn and Bickersteth and M'Cheyne. Tell me of one of all the goodly fellowship of saints and martyrs, who has not had this mark most prominently — he was *a man of prayer.* Depend upon it, prayer is power.

Prayer obtains fresh and continued outpourings of the Spirit. He alone begins the work of grace in a man's heart. He alone can carry it forward and make it prosper. But the good Spirit loves to be entreated. And those who ask most will have most of his influence.

Prayer is the surest remedy against

the devil and besetting sins. That sin will never stand firm which is heartily prayed against. That devil will never long keep dominion over us which we beseech the Lord to cast forth. But then we must spread out all our case before our heavenly Physician, if he is to give us daily relief.

Do you wish to grow in grace and be a devoted Christian? Be very sure, if you wish it, you could not have a more important question than this — **Do you pray?**

I ask whether you pray, because *neglect of prayer is one great cause of backsliding.*

There is such a thing as going back in religion after making a good profession. Men may run well for a season, like the Galatians, and then turn aside after false teachers. Men may profess loudly while their feelings are warm, as Peter did, and then in the hour of trial deny their Lord. Men may lose their first love as the Ephesians did. Men may cool down in their zeal to do good, like Mark the companion of Paul. Men may follow an apostle for a season, and like Demas go back to the world. All these things men may do.

It is a miserable thing to be a back-slider. Of all unhappy things that can befall a man, I suppose it is the worst. A stranded ship, a broken-winged eagle, a garden overrun with weeds, a harp without strings, a church in ruins, all these are sad sights, but a backslider is a sadder sight still. A wounded conscience — a mind sick of itself — a memory full of self-reproach — a heart pierced through with the Lord's arrows — a spirit broken with a load of inward accusation — all this is *a taste of hell*. It is a hell on earth. Truly that saying of the wise man is solemn and weighty, "The backslider in heart shall be filled with his own ways" (Prov. 14:14).

Now what is the cause of most backslidings? I believe, as a general rule, one of the chief causes is neglect of private prayer. Of course the secret history of falls will not be known till the last day. I can only give my opinion as a minister of Christ and a student of the heart. That opinion is, I repeat distinctly, that backsliding generally first begins with *neglect of private prayer.*

Bibles read without prayer; sermons heard without prayer; marriages contracted without prayer; journeys undertaken without prayer; residences chosen without prayer; friendships formed without prayer; the daily act of private prayer itself hurried over, or gone through without heart: these are the kind of downward steps by which many a Christian descends to a condition of spiritual palsy, or reaches the point where God allows him to have a tremendous fall.

This is the process which forms the lingering Lots, the unstable Samsons, the wife-idolizing Solomons, the inconsistent Asas, the pliable Jehoshaphats, the over-careful Marthas, of whom so many are to be found in the church of Christ. Often the simple history of such cases is this: they became *careless about private prayer.*

You may be very sure men fall in private long before they fall in public. They are backsliders on their knees long before they backslide openly in the eyes of the world. Like Peter, they first disregard the Lord's warning to watch and pray, and then like Peter, their strength is gone, and in the hour of temptation they deny their Lord.

The world takes notice of their fall, and scoffs loudly. But the world knows nothing of the real reason. The heathen succeeded in making a well-known

Christian offer incense to an idol, by threatening him with a punishment worse than death. They then triumphed greatly at the sight of his cowardice and apostasy. But the heathen did not know the fact of which history informs us, that on that very morning he had left his bed chamber hastily, and without finishing his usual prayers.

If you are a Christian indeed, I trust you will never be a backslider. But if you do not wish to be a backsliding Christian, remember the question I ask you: **Do you pray?**

I ask, lastly, whether you pray because *prayer is one of the best means of happiness and contentment.*

We live in a world where sorrow abounds. This has always been its state since sin came in. There cannot be sin without sorrow. And until sin is driven out from the world, it is vain for any one to suppose he can escape sorrow.

Some without doubt have a larger cup of sorrow to drink than others. But few are to be found who live long without sorrows or cares of one sort or another. Our bodies, our property, our families, our children, our relations, our servants, our friends, our neighbors, our worldly callings, each and all of these are fountains of care. Sicknesses, deaths, losses, disappointments, partings, separations, ingratitude, slander, all these are common things. We cannot get through life without them. Some day or other they find us out. The greater are our affections the deeper are our afflictions, and the more we love the more we have to weep.

And what is the best means of cheerfulness in such a world as this? How shall we get through this valley of tears with least pain? I know no better means than the regular, habitual practice of

43

taking everything to God in prayer.

This is the plain advice that the Bible gives, both in the Old Testament and the New. What says the psalmist? "Call upon me in the day of trouble, and I will deliver thee, and thou shalt glorify me" (Ps. 50:15). "Cast thy burden upon the Lord, and he shall sustain thee: he shall never suffer the righteous to be moved" (Ps. 55:22). What says the apostle Paul? "Be careful for nothing; but in everything, by prayer and supplication with thanksgiving, let your requests be made known unto God: and the peace of God, which passeth all understanding shall keep your hearts and minds through Christ Jesus" (Phil. 4:6, 7). What says the apostle James? "Is any afflicted among you? let him pray" (James 5:13).

This was the practice of all the saints whose history we have recorded in the Scriptures. This is what Jacob did when he feared his brother Esau. This is what

Moses did when the people were ready to stone him in the wilderness. This is what Joshua did when Israel was defeated before the men of Ai. This is what David did when he was in danger at Keilah. This is what Hezekiah did when he received the letter from Sennacherib. This is what the church did when Peter was put in prison. This is what Paul did when he was cast into the dungeon at Philippi.

The only way to be really happy in such a world as this, is to be ever casting all our cares on God. It is trying to carry their own burdens which so often makes believers sad. If they will tell their troubles to God, he will enable them to bear them as easily as Samson did the gates of Gaza. If they are resolved to keep them to themselves, they will find one day that the very grasshopper is a burden.

There is a friend ever waiting to help us, if we will unbosom to him our sorrow — a friend who pitied the poor and sick and sorrowful, when he was upon earth — a friend who knows the heart of man, for he lived thirty-three years as a man among us — a friend who can weep with the weepers, for he was a man of sorrows and acquainted with grief — a friend who is able to help us, for there never was earthly pain he could not cure. That friend is Jesus Christ. The way to be happy is to be always opening our hearts to him. Oh that we were all like that poor Christian who only answered, when threatened and punished, *"I must tell the Lord."*

Jesus can make those happy who trust him and call on him, whatever be their outward condition. He can give them peace of heart in a prison, contentment in the midst of poverty, comfort in the midst of bereavements, joy on the brink of the grave. There is a mighty fulness in him for all his believing members — a fulness that is ready to be poured out on every one that will ask in prayer. Oh that men would understand that happiness does not depend on outward circumstances, but on the state of the heart.

Prayer can lighten crosses for us, however heavy. It can bring down to our side One who will help us to bear them. Prayer can open a door for us when our way seems hedged up. It can bring down One who will say, "This is the way, walk in it." Prayer can let in a ray of hope when all our earthly prospects seem darkened. It can bring down One who will say, "I will never leave thee, nor forsake thee." Prayer can obtain relief for us when those we love most are taken away, and the world feels empty. It can bring down One who can fill the gap in our hearts with himself, and say to the waves within, "Peace; be still." Oh that men were not so like Hagar in the wilderness, blind to the well of living waters close beside them.

I want you to be happy. I know I cannot ask you a more useful question than this: **Do you pray?**

And now it is high time for me to bring this tract to an end. I trust I have brought before you things that will be seriously considered. I heartily pray God that this consideration may be blessed to your soul.

Let me speak a parting word **to those who do not pray.** I dare not suppose that all who read these pages are praying people. If you are a prayerless person, suffer me to speak to you this day on God's behalf.

Prayerless reader, I can only warn you, but I do warn you most solemnly. I warn you that you are in a position of fearful danger. If you die in your present state, you are a lost soul. You will only rise again to be eternally miserable. I warn you that of all professing Christians you are most utterly without excuse. There is not a single good reason that you can show for living without prayer.

It is useless to say you *know not how to pray*. Prayer is the simplest act in all religion. It is simply speaking to God. It needs neither learning nor wisdom nor book knowledge to begin it. It needs nothing but heart and will. The weakest infant can cry when he is hungry. The poorest beggar can hold out his hand for alms, and does not wait to find fine words. The most ignorant man will find something to say to God, if he has only a mind.

It is useless to say you have *no convenient place* to pray in. Any man can find a place private enough, if he is disposed. Our Lord prayed on a mountain; Peter on the housetop; Isaac in the field; Nathanael under the fig tree; Jonah in the whale's belly. Any place may become a closet, an oratory, and a Bethel, and be to us the presence of God.

It is useless to say you *have no time*. There is plenty of time, if men will employ it. Time may be short, but time is always long enough for prayer. Daniel had the affairs of a kingdom on his hands, and yet he prayed three times a day. David was ruler over a mighty nation, and yet he says, "Evening and morning and at noon will I pray" (Ps. 55:17). When time is really wanted, time can always be found.

It is useless to say you *cannot pray till you have faith and a new heart*, and that you must sit still and wait for them. This is to add sin to sin. It is bad enough to be unconverted and going to hell. It is even worse to say, "I know it, but will not cry for mercy." This is a kind of argument for which there is no warrant in Scripture. "Call ye upon the Lord," saith Isaiah, "while he is near" (Isa. 55:6). "Take with you words, and turn unto the Lord," says Hosea (Hos. 14:1). "Repent and pray," says Peter to Simon Magus (Acts 8:22). If you want faith and a new heart, go and cry to the Lord for them. The very attempt to pray has often been the quickening of a dead soul.

Oh, prayerless reader, who and what are you that you will not ask anything of God? Have you made a covenant with death and hell? Are you at peace with the worm and the fire? Have you no sins to be pardoned? Have you no fear of eternal torment? Have you no desire after heaven? Oh that you would awake from your present folly. Oh that you would consider your latter end. Oh that you would arise and call upon God. Alas, there is a day coming when many shall pray loudly, "Lord, Lord, open to us," but all too late; when many shall cry to the rocks to fall on them and the hills to cover them, who would never cry to God. In all affection, I warn you, beware lest this be the end of your soul. Salvation is very near you. Do not lose heaven for want of asking.

Let me speak **to those who have real desires for salvation,** but know not what steps to take, or where to begin. I cannot but hope that some readers may be in this state of mind, and if there be but one such I must offer him affectionate counsel.

In every journey there must be a first step. There must be a change from sitting still to moving forward. The journeyings of Israel from Egypt to Canaan were long and wearisome. Forty years pass away before they crossed Jordan. Yet there was some one who moved first when they marched from Ramah to Succoth. When does a man really take his first step in coming out from sin and the world? He does it in the day when he first prays with his heart.

In every building the first stone must be laid, and the first blow must be struck. The ark was one hundred and twenty years in building. Yet there was a day when Noah laid his axe to the first tree he cut down to form it. The temple of Solomon was a glorious building. But there was a day when the first huge stone was laid deep in mount Moriah. When does the building of the Spirit really begin to appear in a man's heart? It begins, so far as we can judge, when he first pours out his heart to God in prayer.

If you desire salvation, and want to know what to do, I advise you to go this very day to the Lord Jesus Christ, in the first private place you can find, and earnestly and heartily entreat him in prayer to save your soul.

Tell him that you have heard that he receives sinners, and has said, "Him that cometh unto me I will in no wise cast out." Tell him that you are a poor vile sinner, and that you come to him on the faith of his own invitation. Tell him you put yourself wholly and entirely in his hands; that you feel vile and helpless, and hopeless in yourself: and that except he saves you, you have no hope of being saved at all. Beseech him to deliver you from the guilt, the power, and the consequences of sin. Beseech him to pardon you, and wash you in his own blood. Beseech him to give you a new heart, and plant the Holy Spirit in your soul. Beseech him to give you grace and faith and will and power to be his disciple and servant from this day forever. Oh, reader, go this very day, and tell these things to the Lord Jesus Christ, if you really are in earnest about your soul.

Tell him in your own way, and your own words. If a doctor came to see you when sick you could tell him where you felt pain. If your soul feels its disease indeed, you can surely find something to tell Christ.

Doubt not his willingness to save you, because you are a sinner. It is Christ's office to save sinners. He says himself, "I came not to call the righteous, but sinners to repentance" (Luke 5:32).

Wait not because you feel unworthy. Wait for nothing. Wait for nobody. Waiting comes from the devil. Just as you are, go to Christ. The worse you are, the more need you have to apply to him. You will never mend yourself by staying away.

Fear not because your prayer is stammering, your words feeble, and your language poor. Jesus can understand you. Just as a mother understands the first lispings of her infant, so does the blessed Saviour understand sinners. He can read a sigh, and see a meaning in a groan.

Despair not because you do not get an

answer immediately. While you are speaking, Jesus is listening. If he delays an answer, it is only for wise reasons, and to try if you are in earnest. The answer will surely come. Though it tarry, wait for it. It will surely come.

Oh, reader, if you have any desire to be saved, remember the advice I have given you this day. Act upon it honestly and heartily, and you shall be saved.

Let me speak, lastly, **to those who do pray.** I trust that some who read this tract know well what prayer is, and have the Spirit of adoption. To all such, I offer a few words of brotherly counsel and exhortation. The incense offered in the tabernacle was ordered to be made in a particular way. Not every kind of incense would do. Let us remember this, and be careful about the matter and manner of our prayers.

Brethren who pray, if I know anything of a Christian's heart, you are often sick of your own prayers. You never enter into the apostle's words, "When I would do good, evil is present with me," so thoroughly as you sometimes do upon your knees. You can understand David's words, "I hate vain thoughts." You can sympathize with that poor converted Hottentot who was overheard praying, "Lord, deliver me from all my enemies, and above all, from that bad man — myself." There are few children of God who do not often find the season of prayer a season of conflict. The devil has special wrath against us when he sees us on our knees. Yet, I believe that prayers which cost us no trouble should be regarded with great suspicion. I believe we are very poor judges of the goodness of our prayers, and that the prayer which pleases us *least*, often pleases God *most*. Suffer me then, as a companion in the Christian warfare, to offer you a few words of exhortation. One thing, at least, we all feel: we must pray. We cannot give it up. We must go on.

I commend then to your attention, the importance of *reverence and humility* in prayer. Let us never forget what we are, and what a solemn thing it is to speak with God. Let us beware of rushing into his presence with carelessness and levity. Let us say to ourselves: "I am on holy ground. This is no other than the gate of heaven. If I do not mean what I say, I am trifling with God. If I regard iniquity in my heart, the Lord will not hear me." Let us keep in mind the words of Solomon, "Be not rash with thy mouth, and let not thy heart be hasty to utter anything before God; for God is in heaven, and thou on earth" (Eccl. 5:2). When Abraham spoke to God, he said, "I am dust and ashes." When Job spoke to God, he said, "I am vile." Let us do likewise.

I commend to you the importance of praying *spiritually*. I mean by that, that we should labor always to have the direct help of the Spirit in our prayers, and beware above all things of formality. There is nothing so spiritual but that it may become a form, and this is specially true of private prayer. We may insensibly get into the habit of using the fittest possible words, and offering the most scriptural petitions, and yet do it all by rote without feeling it, and walk daily round an old beaten path. I desire to touch this point with caution and delicacy. I know that there are certain great things we daily want, and that there is nothing necessarily formal in asking for these things in the same words. The world, the devil, and our hearts, are daily the same. Of necessity we must daily go over old ground. But this I say, we must be very careful on this point. If the skeleton and outline of our prayers be by habit almost a form, let us strive that the clothing and filling up of our prayers be as far as possible of the Spirit. As to praying out of a book in our *private* devotions, it is a habit I cannot praise. If we can tell our doctors the state of our bodies without a book, we ought to be able to tell the state of our souls to God. I have no objection to a man using crutches when he is first recovering from a broken limb. It is better to use crutches, than not to walk at all. But if I saw him all his life on crutches, I should not think it matter for congratulation. I should like to see him strong enough to throw his crutches away.

I commend to you the importance

of making prayer *a regular business of life*. I might say something of the value of regular times in the day for prayer. God is a God of order. The hours for morning and evening sacrifice in the Jewish temple were not fixed as they were without a meaning. Disorder is eminently one of the fruits of sin. But I would not bring any under bondage. This only I say, that it is essential to your soul's health to make praying a part of the business of every twenty-four hours in your life. Just as you allot time to eating, sleeping, and business, so also allot time to prayer. Choose your own hours and seasons. At the very least, speak with God in the morning, before you speak with the world: and speak with God at night, after you have done with the world. But settle it in your minds, that prayer is one of the great things of every day. Do not drive it into a corner. Do not give it the scraps and

61

parings of your duty. Whatever else you make a business of, make a business of prayer.

I commend to you the importance of *perseverance* in prayer. Once having begun the habit, never give it up. Your heart will sometimes say, "You have had family prayers: what mighty harm if you leave private prayer undone?" Your body will sometimes say, "You are unwell, or sleepy, or weary; you need not pray." Your mind will sometimes say, "You have important business to attend to today; cut short your prayers." Look on all such suggestions as coming direct from Satan. They are all as good as saying, "Neglect your soul." I do not maintain that prayers should always be of the same length; but I do say, let no excuse make you give up prayer. Paul said, "Continue in prayer, and, "Pray without ceasing." He did not mean that men should be always on their knees, but he did mean that our prayers should be, like the continual burnt offering, steadily persevered in every day; that it should be like seed time and harvest, and summer and winter, unceasingly coming round at regular seasons; that it should be like the fire on the altar, not always consuming sacrifices, but never completely going out. Never forget that you may tie together morning and evening devotions, by an endless chain of short ejaculatory prayers throughout the day. Even in company, or business, or in the very streets, you may be silently sending up little winged messengers to God, as Nehemiah did in the very presence of Artaxerxes. And never think that time is wasted which is given to God. A nation does not become poorer because it loses one year of working days in seven, by keeping the Sabbath. A Christian never finds he is a loser, in the long run, by persevering in prayer.

I commend to you the importance of *earnestness* in prayer. It is not necessary that a man should shout, or scream, or be very loud, in order to prove that he is in earnest. But it is desirable that we should be hearty and fervent and warm, and ask as if we were really interested in what we were doing. It is the "effectual fervent" prayer that "availeth much." This is the lesson that is taught us by the expressions used in Scripture about prayer. It is called, "crying, knocking, wrestling, laboring, striving." This is the lesson taught us by scripture examples. Jacob is one. He said to the angel at Penuel, "I will not let thee go, except thou bless me" (Gen. 32:26). Daniel is another. Hear how he pleaded with God: "O Lord, hear; O Lord, forgive; O Lord, hearken and do; defer not, for thine own sake, O my God" (Dan. 9:19). Our Lord Jesus Christ is another. It is written of him, "In the days of his flesh, he offered up prayers and supplications with strong crying and tears" (Heb. 5:7). Alas, how unlike is this to many of our supplications! How tame and lukewarm they seem by comparison. How truly might God say to many of us, "You do not really want what you pray for." Let us try to amend this fault. Let us knock loudly at the door of grace, like Mercy in *Pilgrim's Progress*, as if we must perish unless heard. Let us settle it in our minds, that cold prayers are a sacrifice without fire. Let us remember the story of Demosthenes the great orator, when one came to him, and wanted him to plead his cause. He heard him without attention, while he told his story without earnestness. The man saw this, and cried out with anxiety that it was all true. "Ah," said Demosthenes, "I believe you *now*."

I commend to you the importance of *praying with faith*. We should endeavor to believe that our prayers are heard, and that if we ask things according to God's will, we shall be answered. This is the plain command of our Lord Jesus Christ: "Whatsoever things ye desire, when ye pray, believe that ye receive them, and ye shall have them" (Mark 11:24). Faith is to prayer what the feather is to the arrow: without it prayer will not hit the mark. We should cultivate the habit of pleading promises in our prayers.

We should take with us some promise, and say, "Lord, here is thine own word pledged. Do for us as thou hast said." This was the habit of Jacob and Moses and David. The 119th Psalm is full of things asked, "according to thy word."

Above all, we should cultivate the habit of expecting answers to our prayers. We should do like the merchant who sends his ships to sea. We should not be satisfied, unless we see some return. Alas, there are few points on which Christians come short so much as this. The church at Jerusalem made prayer without ceasing for Peter in prison; but when the prayer was answered, they would hardly believe it (Acts 12:15). It is a solemn saying of Traill, "There is no surer mark of trifling in prayer, than when men are careless what they get by prayer."

I commend to you the importance of *boldness* in prayer. There is an unseemly familiarity in some men's prayers which I cannot praise. But there is such a thing as a holy boldness, which is exceedingly to be desired. I mean such boldness as that of Moses, when he pleads with God not to destroy Israel "Where-fore," says he, "should the Egyptians speak and say, For mischief did he bring them out, to slay them in the mountains? Turn from thy fierce anger" (Exod. 32:12). I mean such boldness as that of Joshua, when the children of Israel were defeated before men of Ai: "What," says he, "wilt thou do unto thy great name?" (Josh. 7:9). This is the boldness for which Luther was remarkable. One who heard him praying said, "What a spirit, what a confidence was in his very expressions. With such a reverence he sued, as one begging of God, and yet with such hope and assurance, as if he spoke with a loving father or friend." This is the bold-ness which distinguished Bruce, a great Scotch divine of the seventeenth century. His prayers were said to be "like bolts shot up into heaven." Here also I fear we sadly come short. We do not sufficiently realize the believer's privileges. We do not plead as often as we might, "Lord, are we not thine own people? Is it not for thy glory that we should be sanctified? Is it not for thy honor that thy gospel should increase?"

I commend to you the importance of *fullness* in prayer. I do not forget that our Lord warns us against the example of the Pharisees, who, for pretense, made long prayers; and commands us when we pray not to use vain repetitions. But I cannot forget, on the other hand, that he has given his own sanction to large and long devotions by continuing all night in prayer to God. At all events, we are not likely in this day to err on the side of praying *too much*. Might it not rather be feared that many believers in this generation pray *too little*? Is not the actual amount of time that many Christians give to prayer, in the aggregate, very small? I am afraid these questions cannot be answered satisfactorily. I am afraid the private devotions of many are most painfully scanty and limited; just enough to prove they are alive and no more. They really seem to want little from God. They seem to have little to confess, little to ask for, and little to thank him for. Alas, this is altogether wrong. Nothing is more common than to hear believers complaining that they do not get on. They tell us that they do not grow in grace as they could desire. Is it not rather to be suspected that many have quite as much grace as they ask for? Is it not the true account of many, that they have little, because they ask little? The cause of their weakness is to be found in their own stunted, dwarfish, clipped, contracted, hurried, narrow, diminutive prayers. *They have not, because they ask not.* Oh, we are not straitened in Christ, but in ourselves. The Lord says,

"Open thy mouth wide, and I will fill it." But we are like the King of Israel who smote on the ground thrice and stayed, when he ought to have smitten five or six times.

I commend to you the importance of *particularity* in prayer. We ought not to be content with great general petitions. We ought to specify our wants before the throne of grace. It should not be enough to confess we are sinners: we should name the sins of which our conscience tells us we are most guilty. It should not be enough to ask for holiness; we should name the graces in which we feel most deficient. It should not be enough to tell the Lord we are in trouble; we should describe our trouble and all its peculiarities. This is what Jacob did when he feared his brother Esau. He tells God exactly what it is that he fears

(Gen. 32:11). This is what Eliezer did, when he sought a wife for his master's son. He spreads before God precisely what he wants (Gen. 24:12). This is what Paul did when he had a thorn in the flesh. He besought the Lord (II Cor. 12:8). This is true faith and confidence. We should believe that nothing is too small to be named before God. What should we think of the patient who told his doctor he was ill, but never went into particulars? What should we think of the wife who told her husband she was unhappy, but did not specify the cause? What should we think of the child who told his father he was in trouble, but nothing more? Christ is the true bridegroom of the soul, the true physician of the heart, the real father of all his people. Let us show that we feel this by being unreserved in our communications with him. Let us hide no secrets from him. Let us tell him all our hearts.

I commend to you the importance of *intercession* in our prayers. We are all selfish by nature, and our selfishness is very apt to stick to us, even when we are converted. There is a tendency in us to think only of our own souls, our own spiritual conflicts, our own progress in religion, and to forget others. Against this tendency we all have need to watch and strive, and not least in our prayers. We should study to be of a public spirit. We should stir ourselves up to name other names besides our own before the throne of grace. We should try to bear in our hearts the whole world, the heathen, the Jews, the Roman Catholics, the body of true believers, the professing Protestant churches, the country in which we live, the congregation to which we belong, the household in which we sojourn, the friends and relations we are connected with. For each and all of these we should plead. This is the highest charity. He loves me best who loves me in his prayers. This is for our soul's health. It enlarges our sympathies and expands our hearts. This is for the benefit of the church. The wheels of all machinery for extending the gospel are moved by prayer. They do as much for the Lord's cause who intercede like Moses on the mount, as they do who fight like Joshua in the thick of the battle. This is to be like Christ. He bears the names of his people, as their High Priest, before the Father. Oh, the privilege of being like Jesus! This is to be a true helper to ministers. If I must choose a congregation, give me a people that pray.

I commend to you the importance of *thankfulness* in prayer. I know well that asking God is one thing and praising God is another. But I see so close a connection between prayer and praise in the Bible, that I dare not call that true prayer in which thankfulness has no part. It is not for nothing that Paul says, "By prayer and supplication, with thanksgiving, let your requests be made known unto God" (Phil. 4:6). "Continue in prayer, and watch in the same with thanksgiving" (Col. 4:2). It is of mercy that we are not in hell. It is of mercy that we have the hope of heaven. It is of mercy that we live in a land of spiritual light. It is of mercy that we have been called by the Spirit, and not left to reap the fruit of our own ways. It is of mercy that we still live and have opportunities of glorifying God actively or passively. Surely these thoughts should crowd on our minds whenever we speak with God. Surely we should never open our lips in prayer without blessing God for that free grace by which we live, and for that loving kindness which endureth for ever.

Never was there an eminent saint who was not full of thankfulness. St. Paul hardly ever writes an epistle without beginning with thankfulness. Men like Whitefield in the last century, and Bickersteth in our time, abounded in thankfulness. Oh, reader, if we would be bright and shining lights in our day, we must cherish a spirit of praise. Let our prayers be thankful prayers.

I commend to you the importance of *watchfulness over your prayers*. Prayer is that point in religion at which you must be most of all on your guard. Here it is that true religion begins; here it flourishes, and here it decays. Tell me what a man's prayers are, and I will soon tell you the state of his soul. Prayer is the spiritual pulse. By this the spiritual health may be tested. Prayer is the spiritual weatherglass. By this we may know whether it is fair or foul with our hearts. Oh, let us keep an eye continually upon our private devotions. Here is the pith and marrow of our practical Christianity. Sermons and books and tracts, and committee meetings and the company of good men, are all good in their way, but they will never make up for the neglect of private prayer. Mark well the places and society and companions that unhinge your hearts for communion with God and make your prayers drive heavily. *There be on your guard.* Observe narrowly what friends and what employments leave your soul in the most spiritual frame, and most ready to speak with God. *To these cleave and stick fast.* If you will take care of your prayers, nothing shall go very wrong with your soul.

I offer these points for your private consideration. I do it in all humility. I know no one who needs to be reminded of them more than I do myself. But I believe them to be God's own truth, and I desire myself and all I love to feel them more.

I want the times we live in to be praying times. I want the Christians of our day to be praying Christians. I want the church to be a praying church. My heart's desire and prayer in sending forth this tract is to promote a spirit of prayerfulness. I want those who never prayed yet, to arise and call upon God, and I want those who do pray, to see that they are not praying amiss.